Get to know
PHILOSOPHY

A fun, visual guide to the key questions
and big ideas

Written by Rachel Poulton
Illustrated by Gus Scott

Contents

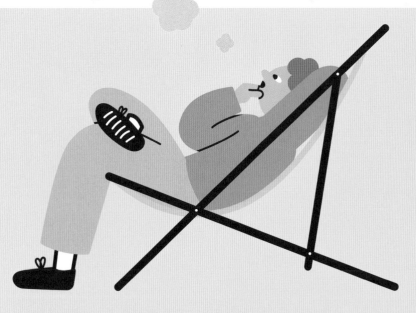

DK | Penguin Random House

Author Rachel Poulton
Illustrator Gus Scott
Editor John Hort
US Editor Margaret Parrish
US Senior Editor Shannon Beatty
Designers Charlotte Jennings, Holly Price, Lucy Sims
Jacket Designer Charlotte Jennings
Managing Editor Jonathan Melmoth
Managing Art Editor Diane Peyton Jones
Production Editor Becky Fallowfield
Production Controller Ben Radley
Deputy Art Director Mabel Chan
Publishing Director Sarah Larter

First American Edition, 2023
Published in the United States by DK Publishing
1745 Broadway, 20th Floor, New York, NY 10019

Copyright © 2023 Dorling Kindersley Limited
DK, a Division of Penguin Random House LLC
23 24 25 26 10 9 8 7 6 5 4 3 2 1
001–325399–Oct/2023

Artwork copyright © Gus Scott, 2023

Published in Great Britain by Dorling Kindersley Limited.

A CIP catalogue record for this book
is available from the British Library.
ISBN: 978-0-7440-8410-8

Printed and bound in China

For the curious
www.dk.com

MIX
Paper | Supporting
responsible forestry
FSC™ C018179

This book was made with Forest Stewardship Council™ certified paper – one small step in DK's commitment to a sustainable future.
For more information go to
www.dk.com/our-green-pledge

What is philosophy?

Philosophy is about seeking wisdom and knowledge. The word comes from an ancient Greek word, *philosophia*, which means "love of wisdom."

Philosophy is active. We "do" philosophy by asking questions about the world and exploring the answers. This helps us to figure out who we are, the nature of the world in which we live, and our place in that world.

Philosophers ask questions such as, "Am I real?" and "What is right?"
?
?

What is a philosopher?

Philosophers are people who are curious about life and the world around them. They think about big ideas and ask lots of questions.

How to be a philosopher

A lot of questions we ask ourselves don't have any clear answers. This means philosophers wonder, discuss, and analyze ideas as they get closer to the truth.

Anyone can be a philosopher!

Reasoning

Philosophers are good at explaining why they think something. They back up ideas with good, solid reasons.

Flexibility

Knowing that you might change your mind about something is also important if you are a philosopher.

Open-mindedness

Philosophers are also open to there being lots of different answers to their questions.

Great philosophers

There have been many, many great philosophers throughout human history, from all over the globe.

Confucius

Confucius was a teacher who taught people all about taking responsibility for their actions.

Lived: 551 BCE–479 BCE
Nationality: Chinese
Expertise: Aesthetics; ethics; politics
Famous writing: *The Analects of Confucius*

Mary Wollstonecraft

Mary Wollstonecraft believed in freedom and equality, especially between men and women.

Lived: 1759–1797
Nationality: British
Expertise: Feminism; politics
Famous writing: *A Vindication of the Rights of Woman*

Changing the world

Thinkers have the power to change the world—no one has influenced Chinese society more than Confucius, while Mary Wollstonecraft is seen as one of the first feminists.

Plato

Plato was a Greek philosopher who believed that there are two worlds: the one that we experience with our senses, and a perfect one that is reached through reasoning. Plato said that true philosophers seek the perfect world, as we will see on the next page.

A physical ice-cream cone

The perfect idea of an ice-cream cone

1

Plato asked us to imagine people tied up in a cave looking at a wall, as if they have been stuck like this all their lives.

2

Behind them there is a fire that casts shadows of everyday life on the wall.

3

The people have only ever seen the wall and the movement of the shadows, and so they think this is real life.

The people think that the shadows they are seeing are "real life."

The shadows move across the wall.

Only a philosophical mind can find out that the shadows are not real.

The allegory of the cave

This story was made up by the philosopher Plato to demonstrate how he believed good philosophers should think.

6

The escapee may try to go back to tell the other captives about the sun. But if the captives don't value truth, they won't believe the escapee.

4

But if someone breaks free, turns around, and sees the shadows are not the real world.

5

A good philosopher is able to escape the cave and find the true source of light—the sun. This represents true knowledge.

A philosopher turns and sees the shadows are being made by objects. But they will look beyond these.

A true philosopher is curious and determined.

The fire is a source of light—but, still, there is more to discover.

The world of ideas

For Plato, the material world (the physical world we experience with our senses) was like the shadows on the wall: an illusion. But the world of ideas, outside the cave, was perfect and unchanging, and that is where all the answers lie.

The allegory of the cave is also a type of thought experiment. You can learn about these on pages 14–15.

Why is there something rather than nothing?
Metaphysics is about finding out what the universe, and everything in it, is. It tries to explain the nature of being.

Do souls exist?
Ontology is the area of metaphysics that is concerned with existence.

Questioning everything

Philosophy covers many different areas. Philosophers have fairly complicated names for these areas, or branches. Most branches interlink and overlap.

Should we always tell the truth?
Ethics, or moral philosophy, is concerned with examining the ideas that are important to live a good life and do the right thing.

Should everyone be treated equally?
Political philosophy is about how society should be organized and who should run communities.

Is there a god?
Philosophy of religion does not just look at beliefs, but also the arguments and concepts behind the beliefs.

How should we think?
Logic is about how philosophers construct valid arguments in order to reach conclusions.

How can we know anything?
Epistemology explores the idea of knowledge. What is it and why is it important?

These questions have been asked for thousands of years.

What is art?
Aesthetics is about considering ideas that help us live well, such as art and beauty.

Philosophy through time

The history of philosophy is vast, as people have questioned the unknown for thousands of years.

Siddhartha Gautama—known as the **Buddha**—was the founder of Buddhism. He questioned how we should live our lives.

Babylonian philosophy can be traced back to the Middle Eastern Mesopotamian region. This was some of the earliest written philosophy, often known as "**wisdom literature**."

3000 BCE

c.500 BCE

1500–400 BCE

1500–400 BCE

Ancient Greece was the birthplace of **Western philosophy**. Socrates, Plato, and Aristotle were Greek thinkers known as the **Titans of Philosophy**, thanks to their huge impact on the subject.

Eastern philosophy originates in ancient India, with the creation of **the Vedas**. These are sacred texts that form the basis of Hindu religion.

500 CE–1300 CE

During the **Medieval period**, religious philosophy flourished. Islamic thinker Ibn Sina, or Avicenna, studied the logical reasons for God's existence.

Focus moved from religion to politics and the natural sciences. This period is known as the **Renaissance**, and it impacted the arts as well as philosophy.

1300–1600

1600–1900

Ideas flourished during the **modern era** of philosophy, particularly on subjects such as metaphysics and politics. Modern philosophy began with a French thinker named **René Descartes**.

THE FUTURE

Philosophy will play an important role in the future, particularly on subjects such as the **environment** and **technology**.

1900–

The modern era ended around 1900, when the **contemporary era** began. Existentialism, feminism, and the philosophy of language are prominent subjects in this era, which continues to this day.

13

Thought experiments

Thought experiments are a way of solving philosophical puzzles. They are imaginary situations made to test an idea and think about the outcomes.

Original idea
Thought experiments start with an idea.

Real-life scenario
A specific scenario is then invented to test the idea.

If there were a pill that could make you live forever, would you take it?

It would be good to live forever.

Produced ideas
What does the real-life scenario say about your original idea?

No—it would mean getting very old, and my friends and family wouldn't live forever. I would not take the pill.

How exciting! Think of all the new things I could see and experience. I would live forever!

The Ship of Theseus

This thought experiment is about identity: what makes a thing what it is?

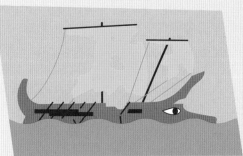

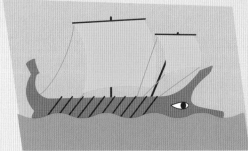

THERE IS AN OLD BOAT. THE MAST BREAKS, PLANKS ROT, AND THE BOLTS AND NAILS HOLDING IT TOGETHER RUST.

OVER TIME, ALL THE ORIGINAL MATERIALS ARE REPLACED WITH NEW ONES. IS THIS STILL THE SAME BOAT?

The Streetcar Problem

This thought experiment explores how we choose the right thing to do.

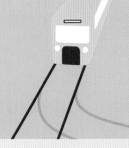

A RUNAWAY STREETCAR IS OUT OF CONTROL, HURTLING ALONG A TRACK.

THERE ARE FOUR PEOPLE ON THE TRACK WHO WILL BE KILLED IF THE STREETCAR HITS THEM.

ON THE OTHER TRACK THERE IS ONE PERSON WHO WOULD BE KILLED IF THE STREETCAR WERE DIVERTED.

UP AHEAD THERE IS A LEVER ON THE TRACK THAT YOU CAN PULL TO DIVERT THE STREETCAR.

What would you do?

Pull the lever and save four lives, but be responsible for the death of one person? Or leave the streetcar to drive on? If you hadn't been there, this would have happened anyway.

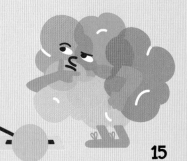

Arguing and logic

Philosophy is about making and examining arguments. Probing and questioning, known as philosophical inquiry, ensures that arguments make sense and that conclusions follow from premises.

Two arguments

All arguments consist of a group of statements, known as "premises" and "conclusions." In a good argument, the premises work together to lead to the conclusion. There are two types of argument: deductive and inductive.

> An inductive argument is when a general conclusion is made from a number of observations.

Inductive argument

Observation:
Five out of 20 of my classmates like olives.

Conclusion:
Five out of 20 of all people like olives.

Building a deductive argument

In a deductive argument, your conclusion follows from the premises. If the premises are true, then your conclusion will also be true. Such an argument is known as a sound argument.

YOU START BUILDING YOUR ARGUMENT WITH A PREMISE THAT IS EITHER TRUE OR FALSE.

> Socrates was a man.

THEN YOU BUILD AN ARGUMENT WITH OTHER PREMISES.

> All men are mortal.

YOUR PREMISES CAN THEN GIVE YOU A SOLID CONCLUSION.

> Therefore, Socrates was mortal.

The Socratic method

In ancient Greece, around 400 BCE, the Greek philosopher Socrates was well-known for arguing. He argued by asking questions. Socrates' style was so effective that it was given its own name: the Socratic method.

Public speaker

Socrates was so committed to arguing as a way to find truth, he never wrote anything down. We only know the stories of Socrates through the writings of his student, Plato.

Posing questions

Socrates wanted to know how people could live good, moral lives. He asked his fellow Athenians questions to try to find truth. Socrates wasn't happy with just a simple answer and followed up his initial question with more questions.

What is love?

Love is desire.

Can you desire something you already have?

No, but you can love something you have.

So is love *really* desire?

Buzz off

Sometimes, Socrates' fellow citizens got angry with all his questions, but he believed it was his job to buzz around, like a gadfly, and create reactions in people. Those reactions could help him in his pursuit of truth.

Wacky thinking

Sometimes, philosophers make mistakes, called fallacies. These can weaken or destroy an argument. It can be tricky to spot them, but the easiest way is to think logically and work through the argument step by step.

Finding fallacies

There are lots of types of fallacies, but here are a few common ones to look for:

Hasty generalization

Watch out when someone is basing a general conclusion on a single piece of evidence.

FOR EXAMPLE...

> I fell off my bike and busted my eardrum, therefore, riding bikes is dangerous.

False cause

Another fallacy is a causal fallacy, in which evidence of a correlation is taken as proof of a causal relationship.

FOR EXAMPLE...

> Every time a rooster crows the sun comes up. The rooster must therefore control the sun.

COCK-A-DOODLE-DOO!

18

False authority

Sometimes people wrongly conclude something is true because it is said by someone in a position of authority.

FOR EXAMPLE...

One day, robots will rule the world. I know it's true because my computer-science teacher said so.

Finding truth

Philosophers try to ensure their premises are true and their conclusions follow on from their premises.

Circular argument

Some arguments go round and round—they are circular and never reach a valid conclusion.

FOR EXAMPLE...

Gold is valuable because it costs a lot of money. Gold costs a lot of money, therefore, it is valuable.

Appeal to ignorance

When someone appeals to ignorance, they are stating that something must be true because it hasn't been proven otherwise.

FOR EXAMPLE...

No one can prove that extraterrestrials exist, so they must not be real.

Philosophical inquiry is the process of finding truth through arguments, logic, and questioning.

Knowledge and thinking

Epistemology is a kind of philosophy all about knowledge and thinking. It is related to philosophy of the mind.

But being an epistemologist does not mean being a know-it-all. It means asking questions, such as, "How do we know things?"

The word epistemology comes from the Greek *episteme*, which means "knowledge," and *logos*, which means "logical discussion."

Knowing and believing

So, what do we mean by knowledge, and what is the difference between knowledge and belief?

You can learn about different religious beliefs on pages 74–75.

The difference

Not all beliefs can be counted as knowledge. A false belief cannot be counted as knowledge because it is false.

Beliefs

We all know that we can believe something is true, but then later discover that it isn't. Beliefs, therefore, can be true or false.

Truth

Truth corresponds to facts. Our beliefs can correspond to facts (and count as knowledge). Or our beliefs can fail to correspond to facts (in which case they don't count as knowledge).

Knowledge

Knowledge, on the other hand, must be true: we cannot know something false (though we can falsely believe we know something that is in fact false).

There is false as well as true belief, but not false as well as true knowledge.

22

Changing thoughts

Knowledge and beliefs can change with time and experience.

Scientists used to believe the sun moved around the Earth.

But in the seventeenth century, the scientist and astronomer Galileo created the telescope and showed that the Earth orbits the sun. Galileo thus proved that the scientists' previous belief was false.

It was never the case that the sun orbited the Earth. But scientists thought it did until they were proven wrong.

If our beliefs can be proven false, can we ever be sure any of them are true? Can we really have knowledge? Can we *know* we have knowledge?

23

How do we learn?

You know more than you did when you were born. But how is that possible? Did you acquire knowledge through observing the world and acting on it, or by using your reason?

Raphael's *The School of Athens*

Learning by reason

Rationalists believe we learn through reasoning: all you need is your mind and your intellect. Descartes was a rationalist, as was Plato.

Some philosophers believe we can't know anything! Find out more on pages 28–29.

No experience needed

Philosophers talk about *a priori* (Latin for "from the earlier") knowledge, which can be learned without direct experience. For instance, mathematics can be learned by logical reasoning alone.

Plato vs. Aristotle

In Raphael's painting *The School of Athens*, Plato points to the heavens, as he believes knowledge comes from reason, not from the physical world. Aristotle gestures to the floor, because he believes knowledge comes from experiencing the physical world.

Plato and Aristotle are at the center of the painting.

Knowledge comes from reason.

Knowledge comes from experience.

Learning by experience

Empiricists believe we learn by experiencing the world around us, conducting experiments and observing. Aristotle, one of Plato's pupils, was an empiricist.

There's nothing like learning by doing!

Real-world experience

A posteriori (Latin for "from the later") knowledge relies upon direct experience. Knowledge is gained only after you have experienced something.

Perception

As we've seen, empiricists believe knowledge is based on how we see, hear, touch, taste, and smell things in the world.

True impressions...

Sometimes we perceive the world correctly.

Imagine you are seeing and hearing the rain on your window. As a result, you form the belief that it is raining. If it *is* raining (rather than someone playing a trick on you), your belief is true. Your belief is justified by your experiences.

Understanding our world

Perception is how we experience the world around us. The problem for philosophers is distinguishing between appearance and reality.

... and false impressions

However, sometimes you might perceive something incorrectly.

When you see a stick partially submerged underwater it can look as if it is broken or bent, but it is actually straight and just appears broken or bent.

A perception problem

Some people see things differently, too. For example, some people see the above image as a duck, while others see a rabbit. So, how much can we really understand the world?

If our senses can be tricked, can we ever trust them?

Read on to pages 28–29 to find out what it can mean if we don't trust our senses.

A computer might feed images into your brain of someone walking.

As a result, you think you are seeing someone walking near you.

Can we know anything?

Some thinkers believe it is impossible to say that we know anything for certain. These philosophers are known as sceptics. They question everything!

Sceptical arguments

Sceptics ask questions such as, "What if life is a dream?"; "How can we trust our senses when they can be tricked?"; and "If everyone's experiences are different, how can there be true knowledge?"

You can see how our senses are easily tricked on pages 26–27.

Brain in a vat

A famous thought experiment asks if we can prove we're not just "brains in a vat" being fed images of our experiences by a computer. Everything we experience could be a clever trick.

A way of life

For some, scepticism is a way of life. The ancient Greek thinker Pyrrho was the first Western philosopher to decide he didn't think anything was either true or false.

A statue of Pyrrho

PYRRHO TRAVELED TO INDIA AND MET SAGES WHO TALKED OF A STATE OF MIND CALLED ATARAXIA, IN WHICH YOU ARE AT PEACE AND FREE FROM ANXIETY.

PYRRHO DISCOVERED THAT HE FELT AT PEACE WHEN HE DID NOT CLING TO KNOWLEDGE OR BELIEFS. HE USED SCEPTICAL ARGUMENTS TO UNDERMINE BELIEFS.

Continual questioning

In the seventeenth century, René Descartes was sceptical about scepticism! He investigated everything he knew to be true by doubting everything. Descartes found that the only thing he could be certain of was that he was thinking, so he must exist in some way.

Descartes famously said: "Cogito, ergo sum" (I think, therefore I am).

29

Philosophy of the mind

Philosophy of the mind explores many interlinked questions.

What is thought?

Is it a form of inner speech, information processing, a reflection of the world around us, or a mixture of all three?

Thinking about thinking

How our minds work, and even what the mind is, is an important branch of philosophy.

What is perception?

Is it more than our five senses? Why does it differ from person to person?

Could a computer have a mind?
Would this change how we viewed our own minds?

Consciousness is being aware of our own thoughts.

Why do we have consciousness?
This question has puzzled philosophers for a long time. It is known as "the hard problem" of consciousness.

What is consciousness?
The seventeenth-century philosopher John Locke defined consciousness as "the perception of what passes in a man's own mind."

What is feeling?
Is a feeling the same as a thought?

Learn how modern-day science has influenced philosophy of the mind on pages 34–35.

Are the mind and

Philosophers have been puzzled by the relationship between our minds and bodies for thousands of years. While some think the mind is separate from the body, others believe they are the same thing.

A separated self
The belief that the mind and body are separate entities is known as dualism.

Who's in control?
When you want to move, your mind relays that message to your body, causing it to move. Dualists argue that because thinking and moving are separate, the mind and body must be separate.

Mind vs. brain
René Descartes believed the mind was distinct from the body, even from the physical brain. Dualism has been influential in science and philosophy for centuries.

Philosophical zombies
The "zombie argument" is a thought experiment designed to argue for dualism.

IMAGINE A ZOMBIE THAT HAS THE SAME BODY AS A HUMAN, BUT NO MIND OR CONSCIOUSNESS.

THE FACT YOU CAN IMAGINE A BEING WITH A BODY BUT NOT A MIND, SUGGESTS THE BODY AND MIND ARE TWO SEPARABLE THINGS.

body separate?

All in the mind

Idealism is the idea that everything only exists as thoughts and ideas. There is no mind and body, only the mind. Irish philosopher George Berkeley came up with the Latin phrase "*esse est percipi*" (to be is to be perceived).

A single self

Monism is the belief that the mind and body are one and the same. Across philosophy, many people have believed this, but not always for the same reason.

Materialists argue that smells and colors that influence our mood are the result of physical processes.

Everything is physical

Materialists argue that only physical things exist. Therefore, thought, feelings, and perceptions are the result of physical processes. The brain is simply a working part of the body.

Monism can be taken further; some philosophers believe the whole universe is just one thing!

The Science of thinking

As science has developed, our understanding of our brains has, too. This has had a big impact on philosophy.

The basics

Many philosophers agree that our minds gather information, which helps us to understand the world around us.

Everyone knows that this object is called an apple. But for many years, no one was certain if people experienced apples in the same way or differently.

Different experiences

Neurobiology is an area of science that helps us understand how we learn. We know that as the brain grows, special cells called neurons connect with each other.

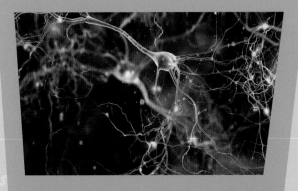

Clever neurons

Everyone's neurons develop in their own unique way, depending on the things a person experiences. So, we know that everyone's mind is different.

Different perceptions

Cognitive psychology, which is the study of how we process information, tells us that individuals also focus on things in their own unique way.

Unique perspectives

It's impossible to compare exactly how each person sees the world, but psychologists have done experiments that prove each individual perceives the world differently.

Applied science

Scientists can pinpoint the areas of the brain that process all our sensory information, including how we experience eating an apple.

One person may turn their attention to the color of the apple, while another focuses on the shape.

When we pick up an apple, we perceive the color, shape, feel, and taste, then all this information is organized in our mind.

35

Time, space, and existence

Some philosophers investigate concepts such as time and space, change, and existence. This area of philosophy is known as metaphysics.

The word metaphysics comes from the Greek words *meta*, meaning "after" or "behind," and *physike*, meaning "physical" or "natural."

Metaphysicians ask questions such as, "What is reality?" and "Why is there something rather than nothing?"

Prehistoric cultures

For many, metaphysical ideas revolved around the concept of a "spirit" world existing alongside the physical world.

This Native American mask was used in ceremonies.

People first settled in the Americas around 30,000 years ago.

Around 3000 BCE, Babylonians told stories of gods and goddesses.

Early ideas

Humans have been thinking about the nature of reality and the principles of being for thousands of years.

Ancient Egyptians explained physical existence as a mixture of Maat (order) and Isfet (chaos).

Myth and space

In ancient Mesopotamia, Egypt, and Central America, people explored ideas of a spirit realm, mythology, and astronomy to understand how the world around them worked and came to be.

This old paper has a drawing of ancient Aztec gods.

Ideas from Earth

Around 550 BCE, Greek philosophers began observing and studying the world around them and came up with various theories unrelated to gods and godesses.

The ancient book *Tao Te Ching* attempts to explain the complex concept of Tao.

Taosim

In ancient China during the fifth and fourth centuries BCE, a philosophy called Taoism (pronounced "dowism") gained popularity. Tao is the great force behind the universe and at the same time it *is* the universe.

Some Greeks thought things were as they were because of four elements: water, air, fire, and earth.

A figurine of Tao Te Ching.

The Vedas are central to the Hindu philosophy and share many ideas with Buddhism and Jainism.

Exploring being

In ancient India, writings known as the Vedas were concerned with exploring the nature of being. Key concepts include: Brahman (reality), Atman (the soul), and Prakriti (the real, physical world).

Linked worlds

Buddhist metaphysical ideas are based on the concept of *dharmas*—the connected mental and physical elements that make up our experiences.

A statue of a Tirthankara, a savior and spiritual teacher in Jainism.

39

Everything is change

Heraclitus believed that everything around us is constantly changing, and that this was a law of nature. Nothing can have a true identity if it is constantly changing. This means that identity is an illusion.

Flow is change

Heraclitus summed up his belief with the statement, "You cannot step in the same river twice." He is saying that just as a river is constantly flowing, so is time constantly changing everything around us.

Do things change?

One of the earliest debates in philosophy comes from two pre-Socratic philosophers: Heraclitus and Parmenides. Both believed the universe could be reduced to one thing. However, they disagreed about what that one thing was.

A constant world

Parmenides took the opposite view of Heraclitus. He reasoned that something could not be created from nothing. Therefore, everything that exists must have always existed, and change is an illusion.

If you were to take a photo of the arrow, it would not show movement, since it captures a single moment.

The arrow paradox

Imagine an arrow in flight. In any single moment, the arrow takes up a single space—it has no motion. The same can be said for any following moments. So how can the arrow move if it has no motion? The change, or motion, is an illusion.

Achilles and the tortoise

Zeno, a pupil of Parmenides, came up with the arrow paradox. He also devised other thought experiments to show change is an illusion.

To overtake the tortoise, Achilles must catch it.

But by the time Achilles reaches the tortoise's starting point, it has moved.

So, whenever Achilles arrives at the point the tortoise has come from, he still has a distance to run to catch it.

IMAGINE ACHILLES IS RACING A TORTOISE, AND THE TORTOISE IS GIVEN A HEAD START.

ALTHOUGH WE MIGHT SEE ACHILLES WIN THE RACE, THIS IS AN ILLUSION. IN THEORY, ACHILLES WOULD NOT CATCH THE TORTOISE, AS CHANGE IS NOT REAL.

Time and space

Thinking about space and time is mind-boggling!
Philosophers have tried to make sense of these
confusing concepts by asking all sorts of questions.

Question of existence

Would space and time exist without
us? This debate takes place between
idealists and realists.

Idealists

Idealists believe time and space
exist only because we perceive them.
Neither space nor time are things on
their own, but features of our minds
as we interpret the world.

Realists

Realists believe time and
space exist independently of
the human mind. Without
humanity, these things would
still exist in the universe.

Are the past and future real?

Time is often separated into three parts: past, present, and future. But are we right to do this?

Philosophers debate which parts of time are real.

M	T	W
The past	**The present**	**The future**
Events in the past have been experienced and can now be known about only by their present effects, especially memories or records made of these experiences.	We know that the present is real because we are experiencing it as it happens.	We can't experience future events, but we can sometimes make predictions about what might happen.

Living in the present
Presentists say that if we were to list everything that exists, the only things on our list would be present things, not things that existed only in the past or that will exist only in the future.

NOW

Building the past
Some philosophers believe each moment in time adds to a **growing block** of space time. Objects that are either past or present should be on our list of existing things, but future things do not (yet) exist.

All moments are equal
Eternalists say that objects, like Plato and homes on the moon, exist now, even if they are not in the same place in space time as we are.

43

Existing

In metaphysics, philosophers distinguish between concrete and abstract objects and agree that almost everything that exists fits into one of these categories.

Concrete things are the things that exist in time and space. They interact with the world and can be sensed.

Concrete

Concrete objects are physical things that exist, such as plants, human beings, animals, and planets.

Buildings

Trees

Insects

Bones

Fruit

Flowers

Earth

Creativity

Time

Love

Knowledge

Emotions

Abstract
Abstract objects are things that don't exist in any particular time or space, such as numbers, colors, and freedom.

Numbers

Colors

Evolution of terms

"Concrete" and "abstract" started as a grammatical distinction, "blue" being concrete, while "blueness" is abstract. The philosopher John Locke talked of abstract and concrete ideas. It is only in modern times that philosophers have talked about concrete and abstract objects.

Some things, such as shadows and holes, are neither abstract nor concrete.

In the game
The game of soccer exists in the abstract (soccer refers to the rules, the tactics, teams, and much more), but a soccer game, played by human players, with a soccer ball, on a field, exists in the concrete.

Are we free?

Why do we do certain things? When you eat something, is it because you choose to, or is it caused by other factors you don't control, such as hunger, or the temperature outside?

THIS WAY

THAT WAY

As free agents, we can decide what we do when confronted with events.

Choose a path

The idea of free will says that individuals are in control: we are free to think and act in the way that we choose.

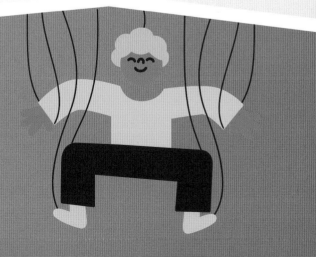

Problems with free will

Not everyone agrees we have free will. For instance, some argue that if there is something causing us to make the choices, then we cannot be acting with free will.

Cause and effect

Determinism says that we don't have free will. Everything that we think and do is caused by past events in accordance with the laws of nature. Determinists argue that all human actions are just following the laws that control the physical world.

Everything that happens is just like a falling line of dominoes—predetermined.

The Big Bang

Determinists believe everything happens as a result of an unbroken chain of events that can be tracked back to a first cause. Most people agree that the universe started with the Big Bang, but what caused the Big Bang?

Problems with determinism

If we don't have free will, can we be held responsible for our actions? Is it possible that a mixture of free will and determinism are true, and that our will can effect events that were always likely to happen?

Humans being

During the nineteenth century, some philosophers promoted the idea that we create ourselves by choosing our own actions. These philosophers were known as existentialists.

Personal responsibility

Existentialism is all about realizing that we each have free will, free choice, and individual responsibility for our actions. It is up to each person to live their life however they want.

> Our choices are individual and unique—like our fingerprints.

A statue of Søren Kierkegaard in Copenhagen, Denmark.

The first existentialist

One philosopher, Søren Kierkegaard, believed in complete, individual free will, but acknowledged this could be very scary. Although it may cause anxiety and despair, Kierkegaard believed feelings were a big part of being a human.

The existentialist movement

During the middle of the twentieth century, a group of existential philosophers and writers gathered in Paris, France, and discussed ideas around human existence.

Jean-Paul Sartre

Jean-Paul Sartre said a person simply exists, and that it is our choices and actions that make us who we are.

Lived: 1905–1980
Nationality: French
Expertise: Existentialism, politics
Famous writing: *Nausea*

Disappointment and enjoyment

Sartre said it was important to make meaningful choices in life and accept that sometimes things don't work out quite how we hoped. Life might be disappointing at times, but if we are aware of that, it can still be meaningful and enjoyable.

Simone de Beauvoir

Simone de Beauvoir was an existentialist and a feminist. She had a huge influence on feminism and feminist theory.

Lived: 1908–1986
Nationality: French
Expertise: Existentialism, feminism, politics
Famous writing: *The Second Sex*

Being a woman

De Beauvoir said that society tells us what a woman is and should be, but that these are just ideas that have been created by people. Women should therefore reject the stereotypes of being a woman and assert their free will to become what and who they are.

"One is not born but becomes a woman."
–Simone de Beauvoir

Key words

Language is essential. We use language to communicate our thoughts to others. Some philosophers argue that thought would be impossible without language.

Wording the world

We use language to describe the world around us. In English, a sentence such as "the car is red" represents a situation in which a particular thing in the world (the car) has a certain property (the property of being red in color).

Being understood

Words are important when it comes to knowledge and understanding.

TWO PEOPLE WHO SHARE A LANGUAGE WILL EACH KNOW WHAT THE OTHER MEANS WHEN THEY USE THE COMMON WORDS OF THAT LANGUAGE.

YET A PERSON WHO DOES NOT SHARE THAT LANGUAGE WILL HEAR ONLY MEANINGLESS NOISE.

Choose your words

Philosophers are very careful with language, because it is only by understanding each others' words that we understand each others' arguments. Philosophy of language is devoted to understanding how words have meaning and how these relate to the world.

The British philosopher Bertrand Russell (left) and his student Ludwig Wittgenstein (right) believed that language is a major cause of philosophical confusion. Therefore, studying and understanding language is an important part of philosophy.

Shared meanings

Wittgenstein recognized the importance of *shared* meanings. He argued that a private language, a language no one else could understand, would be impossible.

????

What do you mean?

Meaning is importantly related to truth. "The cat is on the mat" refers to a situation in the world. If the world is as the sentence states it to be, then the sentence is true. If it is not, then the sentence is false.

51

Right, wrong, and rules

Moral philosophy, also known as ethics, studies whether what we do is right, or wrong, or neither.

Some philosophers believe that morality is a system of rules. Other philosophers disagree.

The word ethics comes from the ancient Greek word *ēthikós*, meaning "relating to one's character."

Rules and morals

One question asked by moral philosophers is: what is the relationship between morality and rules?

Rules

RULES ARE ESSENTIAL FOR THE SMOOTH RUNNING OF ANY SOCIETY OR COMMUNITY. UNLESS THERE IS A SET OF RULES THAT ALL COMMUNITY MEMBERS ABIDE BY, THE COMMUNITY WILL NOT WORK EFFECTIVELY.

Rules on behavior can come from many sources, such as parents, school, government, or religion.

Morality and society

Morality is about deciding what is right and wrong behavior. To behave morally is to do the right thing, especially to others in a community.

Wrong rules

There can be unjust rules—rules that are not morally right—and rules that should exist, but don't. Rules seem, therefore, to be based on, but not identical to, morality.

RIGHT

WRONG

Are there any rules that you think are unfair?

What would life be like with no rules?

The way to behave

Aristotle believed that all moral decisions have to be made in relation to a particular situation. If Aristotle is correct, rules have a much less important place in morality than many people think.

Aristotle thought the purpose of morality is to become good, not to know what's good.

55

Moral frameworks

There are three major ideas about how we should understand morality. Each of the three ideas can be used to answer questions of what actions are right or wrong.

Think consequences

Consequentialism is a theory that states the morality of an action is determined by its outcomes. The most famous form of consequentialism is utilitarianism.

Consequentialists believe the outcome of an action is important.

For the many

Utilitarianism states that an action is right if it produces the greatest happiness for the greatest number of people.

Rules for life

Deontology states that some types of action are morally required or forbidden, whatever the consequences. For example, it is not right to kill a person even if doing so will save the lives of others.

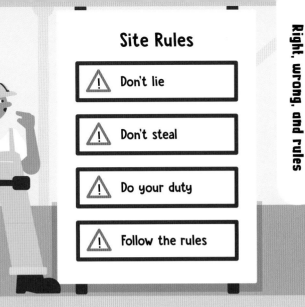

Site Rules

⚠	Don't lie
⚠	Don't steal
⚠	Do your duty
⚠	Follow the rules

A moral self

Virtue theory focuses on the person rather than actions. It states that we must acquire virtues such as courage, honesty, and kindness, and that a life lived in accordance with these virtues is the only good life.

Questions answered

Using each moral framework, philosophers can find answers to whether actions are moral.

For instance, a believer in virtue theory would be unlikely to throw a party when they are working, since it is dishonest.

But a consequentialist may say it is right, as long as the work is still completed and no harm is done!

57

Helping those in need

Australian philosopher Peter Singer believes that it is everyone's moral duty to help others. He came up with a thought experiment to illustrate this dilemma.

No. Yikes!

What would you do in these scenarios?

You come across a young child struggling in a pond. They need help, but if you wade in you will ruin your new shoes. Do you wade in and help the child in trouble?

Decisions, decisions

Every day we use morals to guide our decisions. Applied ethics is a branch of philosophy that deals with real-life moral problems. It explores the right and wrong things a person could do and tries to explain how they should act.

Yes. Most people agree that sacrificing a pair of shoes to save a life is good.

No. Someone else will probably help. I can save my new shoes.

No. I have to look after people in my own neighborhood. I can't help people on the other side of the world, too.

What about if there are other people walking past who could help. Is it still your responsibility to rescue the child?

What if this child is in another country? You can help the child by donating money to charity.

Yes. It's still my responsibility to help.

Yes. It makes no difference where they are. Saving a child's life is a good thing to do.

Finally, as millions of children's lives are at risk every day all over the world, are you morally obliged to donate to charity? How much? The value of a new pair of shoes?

Rules to live by

Most philosophers agree that following a shared morality, cooperating, and promoting the common good is positive for human beings and for societies all over the world.

The Golden Rule is simple: do not do unto others what you would not want others to do unto you.

The Golden Rule

Confucius came up with a rule to guide us on how to live a moral life. This moral principle is about being kind, fair, and loving toward others, because this is how you would expect others to treat you.

A strong foundation
The Golden Rule has formed the basis of many religions and the social order in societies all over the world for thousands of years.

Common values

There are some rules that are common all around the world in many different societies. But are they always right?

1. GROUP LOYALTY: HELP THOSE AROUND YOU

2. TOLERANCE: ACCEPT THOSE WHO HAVE DIFFERENT BELIEFS OR BEHAVIORS FROM YOU

Should we tolerate people who are themselves intolerant?

3. ENGAGE: UNDERSTAND HOW YOU CAN HELP SOCIETY

4. RESPECT: DEFER TO AUTHORITY

Should we respect authority if leaders are behaving in an immoral way? What if an authority figure tells you to break one of these other rules?

5. FAIRNESS: SHARE RESOURCES FAIRLY

6. PROPERTY RIGHTS: RESPECT THINGS BELONGING TO OTHERS

What if someone bought property with money they made dishonestly?

61

Early politics

Humans have always had ideas about how societies should be run. If people live together in groups, small or large, they have to be very organized.

Learn more about Confucius's Golden Rule on page 60.

The Confucian way

Confucius had clear ideas about how Chinese society should work. Alongside the Golden Rule, he included Chinese traditional values of caring for others, loyalty, and respect for family and friends in his political ideas.

Leading by example

Confucius believed rulers shouldn't just tell people what to do, they should lead by example. He said that being a good person and developing the self was important morally, socially, and politically.

If everyone behaves in a good and moral way toward each other, the result is social order, stability, and peace.

Plato's society

Plato believed society should be divided into three parts. He wrote about these ideas in his most famous work, *The Republic*.

Plato believed there should be honest and trustworthy **philosopher-kings** at the head of state.

Also known as the **guardians**, philosopher-kings are trained in justice and order.

A fair society?

Although Athens was a democracy at the time, Plato didn't think everyone should vote. He believed only the philosophical elite were qualified to vote.

Auxiliaries are soldiers who enforce the rules of the leaders.

For Plato, the ideal society mirrored the ideal soul: reason should rule the individual, too.

Producers and workers make the goods and services in society.

63

Playing politics

Political philosophy focuses on issues having to do with society and government. It is concerned with big ideas related to morality, such as fairness, freedom, and justice.

Social animals

Aristotle said human beings are "social animals" who choose to live in communities. To live in society is to be part of something bigger than us, and so we develop rules to ensure people live in harmony with each other.

Some philosophers disagree about why we have rules.

Some philosophers believe that if we didn't have rules, or laws, people would behave selfishly and there would be chaos.

Other philosophers believe that humans are naturally good and cooperative and want to treat each other well, but that we still need laws to protect our rights if there is a dispute.

Creating equality

Two very significant philosophers believed that rules in society should be used to create equality.

Protecting rights

John Locke believed that people are born equal, and that they should elect leaders to a government, whose job it is to make rules that protect the rights of individuals.

Jean-Jacques Rousseau

Jean-Jacques Rousseau was a musician and philosopher whose writing on humanity and freedom changed the landscape of Europe.

Lived: 1712–1778
Nationality: Swiss
Expertise: Politics, economics
Famous writing: *The Social Contract*

John Locke

John Locke argued that every individual has a "natural right" to life, liberty, and property.

Lived: 1632–1704
Nationality: British
Expertise: Politics, metaphysics
Famous writing: *Two Treatises of Government*

Skewed system

Jean-Jacques Rousseau argued that laws are made by rich people to protect their wealth, and that laws limit individuals' freedom. Rousseau believed that rules should be made according to the "general will"— what most people want.

Revolution!

A big turning point for political philosophy and countries around the world was the Age of Reason, also known as the Enlightenment. This period was a time of extreme scientific revolution, as well as political change.

ENLIGHTENMENT THINKERS STOOD FOR POLITICAL FREEDOM, CRITICAL THINKING...

For liberty!

Enlightenment ideas triggered the Revolutionary War, as people living in the now-United States wanted freedom and independence from the British government. These British colonies obtained independence from the British and set up the first nation-state based on liberal democracy.

Freedom fighting

The Boston Tea Party was a protest against British taxes, where rebels threw British-imported tea into Boston Harbor. It is one of the actions that started the Revolutionary War.

Liberalism

FROM THE LATIN WORD LIBER, MEANING "FREE", IT STARTS WITH THE IDEA THAT ALL PEOPLE ARE BORN EQUAL.

... RELIGIOUS TOLERANCE, SCIENTIFIC INQUIRY, FREEDOM OF THOUGHT...

... AND THE PURSUIT OF HAPPINESS.

Change in the air

During the seventeenth and eighteenth centuries, philosophers were calling for society to be more equal and based on individual liberty, rather than everyone being told how to live by the Church or a ruling monarch.

Enlightenment ideas inspired two important revolutions in different parts of the world.

For democracy!

The French Revolution, which began in 1789, was a result of social, political, and economic unrest in France, and anger at the ruling royals. Revolutionaries called for freedom, equality, and fraternity. The king was overthrown, and a French Republic was declared in 1792, based on democratic ideals.

Democracy

SYSTEM OF GOVERNMENT IN WHICH THE PUBLIC VOTES FOR ITS LEADERS.

On July 14, 1789, revolutionaries stormed a fortress and political prison known as the Bastille, which represented royal rule in Paris. It was a key point in the transfer of power from the king to the revolutionaries.

Politics influences and encompasses many things all around the world.

The political spectrum

The political spectrum shows how different political beliefs relate to one another. The most common spectrum is shown as left to right.

Far left

Communism
The belief that all people should be equal: there are no social classes or differences in wealth.

Equality at all cost
Everything is communally owned. All wealth is redistributed among all people, so there is no freedom to own things or make lots of money.

Left

Socialism
States that it is the government's responsibility to make society fairer.

Equality at some cost
Everyone pays taxes, but rich people pay more than less-wealthy people. Everyone works together as a society, while having the freedom to own things and make money.

Ever since the Enlightenment, people have come up with different ways of organizing societies. These ideas are usually placed somewhere on the political spectrum.

| Center | Right | Far right |

Liberalism

Interference from government is limited— it is there to protect people's freedoms.

Equal opportunity

Equality of opportunity is important: everyone should work hard and make something of their lives.

Conservatism

Promotes traditional values and ideas. It favors freedom of individuals.

Hard work pays off

People should work hard and be productive. Taxes are low, so inequality can occur between the rich and the less wealthy.

Fascism

People do not have equal rights. There is usually one leader, called a dictator.

Huge inequality

Leaders often discriminate against people based on their race, social class, religion, or ethnicity.

Crime and punishment

We have seen that rules are important in a society. But what should be the punishment for breaking them?

Protecting the people

At your school, you might have class rules for everyone to follow, which keep the teacher and pupils safe and happy. Similarly, societies have laws that help to protect people.

Justice system

Justice is when something is morally correct or fair. A justice system exists to ensure that people who have done something wrong are punished. Consequences might be paying a fine or going to prison.

What ifs?
Justice is very complicated. There are many things to consider when making laws.

What if the punishment doesn't stop people from breaking the rules again?

What if the rules aren't fair?

What if one person thinks the rules are fair but another doesn't?

Is it okay to break the law in some situations?

What if the punishment is unfair?

If it is okay to break the law in some situations, can some of the things we think are bad sometimes be right?

What if I hurt someone because they were trying to hurt me or my family?

Questioning the system
French philosopher Michel Foucault argued that crime and justice is decided by those people in power and so is very unfair. He believed that people in authority used their power to discipline and control people.

Justice must always question itself.

Michel Foucault influenced many areas of study in the twentieth century, including psychology, sociology, and criminology.

Religion, art, and beauty

Humans have been partaking in both religion and art for tens of thousands of years.

Given their importance to the human experience and our culture, it is no surprise that these subjects are of great interest to philosophers.

Philosophers examine what makes both art and religion special.

Absolutely not!

Agnosticism

This is the view that the existence of God or gods is unknowable because it is impossible to prove or disprove scientifically.

Atheism

Atheists don't believe in the existence of deities, or gods. They argue that there is no scientific evidence that God or gods exist.

Different beliefs

When it comes to religion, there are many gods, texts, and traditions. However, almost everyone's beliefs can be grouped into one of these categories.

I believe in something...

Arguments theists use to try to prove God exists can be found on page 78.

Theism
This is the belief that a supreme being or deities exist.

Monotheism
Monotheists believe that only one deity exists. Monotheistic religions include Christianity, Judaism, Islam, and Sikhism.

Christianity has one God.

Polytheism
Polytheists believe there is more than one god. Ancient Greek and Egyptian religions were polytheistic, as is Hinduism.

The ancient Egyptians believed in many gods.

The history of religion

All societies seem to have religions of some sort. Some people believe religion developed as our human ancestors evolved to live in groups.

Religion has changed a lot throughout human history.

Archeologists have found prehistoric sculptures that suggest religion existed around the time of the first modern humans.

40,000–8000 BCE

A carved statue of a "lion man," which some historians believe is evidence of religion.

8000–1500 BCE

The first polytheistic religions appeared around this time, including Hinduism.

A sculpture of Vishnu, one of the main deities of Hinduism.

Social evolution

Some people believe religion has helped humans evolve by creating close social groups, as well as a clear set of rules to live by.

1500 BCE–500 CE

Zoroastrianism was one of the first monotheistic religions to appear. It was followed by Buddhism, Judaism, and Christianity.

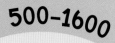

A religious symbol of Zoroastrianism

1600–

The world is full of different religious beliefs.

500–1600

Islam was born. Along with Christianity, it spread across much of the world.

The Quba Mosque in Medina, Saudi Arabia.

Christianity, Islam, and Hinduism have become the world's most popular religions. But the number of atheists and agnostics is growing.

Religious morals

Religion often acts as a way of directing people morally.

It tries to steer people away from actions that result in negative feelings, such as anger and jealousy.

Religions emphasize the importance of positive emotions, such as love and happiness.

Can we prove that God exists?

Arguments for...
These are the main arguments for the existence of God.

A perfect being
One argument states that God must exist, simply because we can have the idea that a perfect being exists. If this being didn't exist, it wouldn't be perfect. This is known as the **ontological** argument.

The root cause
Some people argue that God must exist, otherwise what caused everything? Something can't come from nothing, so something must have created it. This is known as the **cosmological** argument.

Amazing nature
Nature is so perfect, it must have been created by a supremely intelligent being, God. This is known as the **teleological** argument.

But is nature always perfect?

One of the oldest and biggest debates in philosophy is whether we can prove if a god exists. There are many arguments for and against.

Arguments against...

These are the main arguments against the existence of God.

The problem of evil

This argument questions how evil and suffering can exist if God is both all-loving and all-powerful. Could God not just stop it?

What caused the cause?

If God created the universe, then who created God? Science tells us that everything comes from something, and it is science that will answer how the universe came to be.

No proof

No evidence has ever been found to prove the existence of a God, or gods. Historical evidence and people saying they have experienced divine things are inconsistent.

Russell's teapot is a thought experiment by Bertrand Russell. He said that if he told everyone there was a tiny teapot orbiting the sun, no one could disprove it, but that does not mean people should believe him—it is up to Russell to prove it. Likewise, Russell said it's up to theists to prove that God exists, not atheists.

Religion without beliefs

We often think of religion being dependent on a God or many gods, but some people follow religions without a god. These are known as nontheistic religions.

A new New Testament

Russian author Leo Tolstoy wrote his version of the New Testament, the second part of Christianity's holy book. Published in 1902, *The Gospel in Brief* excluded the supernatural elements of the story of Jesus and focused on his teachings, or philosophy.

The Sermon on the Mount is a story from the New Testament in which Jesus leads his many followers up a mountain in order to begin a speech.

Sermon on the Mount

Tolstoy believed the core of Christianity can be found in Jesus' Sermon on the Mount, which emphasizes the moral teachings of Christianity rather than the supernatural elements of religion.

Path to enlightenment

Buddhists follow a path in life to end suffering. It is known as The Noble Eightfold Path.

You can read more about Buddhism on page 12.

Nirvana is the highest state of being. It is "outside" any idea of God, or gods.

Nirvana is freedom from the cycle of pursuing things that bring suffering—greed, anger, and delusion.

Buddhists meditate to reach a state called Nirvana, which does not depend on a god.

So do you need to believe in a god to be a Christian or a Buddhist?

The Eightfold Path emphasizes kindness and self-reflection through meditation.

What is art?

Art can take many, many forms, such as a painting, a story, a dance, or a film. Art can also be aspects of nature. If it can evoke emotion, it can probably be called art.

Philosophers have long debated, and continue to debate, an exact definition of art!

Leonardo da Vinci's *Mona Lisa* is a very famous artwork.

Ballet is a kind of performance art.

Questions of art

Why do people make art?

Art can be an expression of thoughts, emotions, desires, or experiences. When people can't explain things in words, they can create art to help them express what they mean.

A peace mural in Northern Ireland.

Graffiti artist Banksy is known for his political works, such as *The Flower Thrower*.

Can art change the world?

In addition to showing what an artist is observing, such as landscape art, art can be political and aim to highlight social or economic injustices. As a result, it can inspire change in the world.

Art that results in a strong emotional response or gets its message across is often considered successful.

Aesthetics is the name given to the area of philosophy that considers beauty, taste, and the philosophy of art. There are a few key questions in aesthetics.

Is all art equal?

Art is subjective, which means it is up to each individual viewer to decide whether or not they like it. It is normal to like some types of art more than others, but other people may disagree!

Judging beauty

Beauty is a word we use to describe something that is enjoyable to our senses, such as a landscape or a piece of music. But why do we enjoy beautiful things?

Objective vs. subjective

Does beauty depend upon who is looking? Or are things objectively beautiful—is it a matter of truth, rather than taste?

Perfect beauty

Plato believed that beauty exists as a form—a concept that is perfect and exists beyond our senses. Therefore, beauty is an **objective** quality; things we experience have the quality of beauty in them, so it is not a matter of opinion.

Subjective and universal

German philosopher Immanuel Kant said that things are beautiful because we all understand them to be, and there doesn't need to be a reason. Kant believed that beauty can be both subjective and **universal**—some things are beautiful to everyone.

In the eye of the beholder

Many people argue that beauty is **subjective**—it is up to the individual to decide what they think is beautiful.

Beauty depends on how something interacts with our senses.

Aesthetic experience

Sometimes, people are so overwhelmed by something beautiful that it can create a strong physical or mental response. Your heart might beat faster, or you might feel in awe. This is known as an aesthetic experience.

The philosopher John Dewey said that aesthetic experiences are the richest of all experiences.

The beauty of philosophy

Philosophy, and the search for knowledge and truth, is a beautiful activity to many thinkers. But the true beauty of philosophy is that is useful in everyday life.

Critical thinking

Philosophy not only helps us solve problems, but it also helps us to question problems that are presented to us.

Decision-making

By studying philosophy, we can make fairer and more just decisions.

A key concept

Beauty is traditionally seen as one of life's virtues, alongside goodness, truth, and justice. Together, these concepts remain key pillars of philosophy.

Understanding

Philosophy helps us understand the world, and our place in it.

Can you think of any situations in your life where philosophy may be able to help?

Quiz

It's time to put your philosophy knowledge to the test!

1. Who said "I think, therefore I am"?

a. Socrates
b. Confucius
c. René Descartes
d. Michel Foucault

2. What is the name of Plato's famous allegory?

a. The cart
b. The cave
c. The horse
d. The chariot

3. Which is a concrete object?

a. Banana
b. Happiness
c. Red
d. Time

4. What is the name of Confucius's most important rule?

a. The Silver Rule
b. The Bronze Rule
c. The Golden Rule
d. The Copper Rule

5. What is another name for the philosophy of art?

a. Metaphysics
b. Epistemology
c. Ethics
d. Aesthetics

1. Epistemology explores the idea of knowledge.

2. Not all beliefs can be counted as knowledge.

3. Fallacies are a sign of a good argument.

4. Everyone believes time would exist without humans.

5. A sceptic believes we can know everything.

6. Utilitarianism is about producing the best outcome for the most people.

7. Polytheists believe there are many gods.

TRUE or FALSE

Famous philosophers

Here are some of the best-known philosophers throughout time.

Confucius (c.551–c.479 BCE)
Chinese philosopher and politician, whose teachings have influenced many cultures.

Heraclitus (c.540–c.480 BCE)
Ancient Greek philosopher who had a strong impact on early metaphysical debates.

Parmenides (c.515–c.445 BCE)
Ancient Greek philosopher, who is often considered the fount of ontology (the philosophy of being).

Socrates (c.470–399 BCE)
Athenian philosopher who is seen as the founder of Western philosophy. We know him through the accounts of other writers, particularly his student Plato.

Plato (c.424 BC–348 BCE)
Athenian philosopher who founded the Academy, a school in Greece that some say was the world's first university. Plato's dialogues are still taught today.

Aristotle (384–322 BCE)
Ancient Greek philosopher, often known as the father of science. A student of Plato, Aristotle went on to found his own school, called the Lyceum, in Athens.

Pyrrho (c.360–c.272 BCE)
Ancient Greek philosopher who is seen as the first European sceptic philosopher.

Zeno (c.334–c.262 BCE)
Ancient Greek philosopher and the first Stoic, an area of philosophy that seeks goodness and peace of mind through living a virtuous life.

Ibn Sina (980–1037 CE)
Persian thinker, physician, and astronomer. He is known as a polymath (someone who has a wide range of detailed knowledge).

Thomas Aquinas (1225–1274)
Italian thinker and theologian who embraced many Aristotelian ideas and united them with Christianity. Aquinas was a key thinker during the medieval period in Europe.

René Descartes (1596–1650)
French philosopher, mathematician, and scientist. He is known as the father of modern philosophy because of his huge impact on the direction of the subject.

John Locke (1632–1704)

English philosopher and key part of the Enlightenment movement. His influences on political philosophy and philosophy of the mind are still relevant today.

George Berkeley (1685–1753)

Anglo-Irish thinker who advanced the idea of "immaterialism," the idea that objects cannot exist without being perceived.

David Hume (1711–1776)

Scottish thinker who contributed ideas on the self, free will, and scepticism.

Jean-Jacques Rousseau (1712–1778)

Genevan thinker and musician whose ideas on political philosophy progressed the French Revolution.

Immanuel Kant (1724–1804)

German philosopher who wrote on epistemology, metaphysics, ethics, and aesthetics. His long and detailed works have made him one of the most important philosophers on this list!

Mary Wollstonecraft (1759–1797)

English thinker, seen as one of the founding feminist philosophers. Her work supporting equality and criticizing traditional ideas of womanhood is still important today.

Georg Hegel (1770–1831)

German philosopher who had a big influence across a range of topics, including epistemology, metaphysics, politics, aesthetics, and religion.

Arthur Schopenhauer (1788–1860)

German atheist thinker who was one of the first Western philosophers to explore and agree with ideas in Eastern philosophy.

Søren Kierkegaard (1813–1855)

Danish thinker and poet who wrote critiques of organized religion. His emphasis on the single individual means he is the first existentialist philosopher.

Karl Marx (1818–1883)

German thinker, best known for his work *The Communist Manifesto*. Marx's political and philosophical ideas have shaped the politics of our world today.

Friedrich Nietzsche (1844–1900)

German thinker known for beautiful writings. Having written extensively about religion and morality, his work has influenced many books and films.

Bertrand Russell (1872–1970)

Welsh philosopher who had a huge impact on logic, language, epistemology, and metaphysics.

Ludwig Wittgenstein (1889–1951)

Austrian philosopher, who is seen by many as the greatest thinker of the twentieth century. His areas of expertise were logic, language, mathematics, and philosophy of the mind.

Martin Heidegger (1889–1976)

German philosopher, who wrote on metaphysics and existentialism.

Jean-Paul Sartre (1905–1980)

French thinker, who was a key figure in the philosophy of existentialism.

Simone de Beauvoir (1908–1986)

French existentialist philosopher, writer, and feminist. She has had a big impact on feminist theory.

Michel Foucault (1926–1984)

French philosopher and writer who influenced many areas of learning, including psychology, sociology, criminology, and literature.

Glossary

aesthetics a branch of philosophy concerned with beauty and art

agnosticism the belief that existence of a divine being is unknown

allegory a story that can be interpreted to reveal a hidden meaning

atheism the belief that there is no divine being

communism a social system in which all property is owned by the community

conclusion a judgment reached by reasoning

consequentialism a moral theory that states an action is good or bad depending on the outcome

conservatism the political view that favors traditional ideas and people being able to own things

deductive argument if the premises of such an argument are true, the conclusion will be true as well

democracy a system of government in which the people vote for those who decide how society should be run

deontology an ethical theory that states the morality of an action is right or wrong depending on a set of rules, rather than the consequences

determinism the idea that all events are determined by previously existing causes

dualism the theory that the mind and body are separate

empiricism the theory that all knowledge is based on experience gained from the senses

epistemology the philosophical study of the nature, origin, and limits of knowledge

ethics the branch of philosophy that deals with morality

existentialism the belief that an individual person is free and responsible for their own actions

externalism the belief that the content of a thought is partly dictated by the environment

fallacy a bad argument that looks like a good one

fascism a political ideology in which society is run by a dictatorial leader through the suppression of all opposition

feminism the promotion of equality for women and individual female rights

hedonism a moral theory that states something is right or wrong depending on the amount of pleasure it creates

hierarchy a ranked system of social order in a community

idealism the idea that reality exists in the mind rather than material objects

inductive argument an argument based on experience rather than pure reason

liberalism a political philosophy based on the rights of the individual and equality

logic reasoning that is done according to strict rules of validity

materialism the theory that nothing exists except matter

metaphysics the branch of philosophy that hopes to identify the most universal characteristics of reality

monism a theory or doctrine that denies the idea of dualism

monotheism the belief in a single god

objective a judgment that is not influenced by personal feelings or opinions

ontology the branch of philosophy that looks at the nature of being

paradox a statement that seems to contradict itself, but also seems true

perception the ability to become aware of something through our senses

polytheism the belief in more than one god

premise the basis of an argument or theory

presentism the theory that only the present is real

rationalism the theory that reason, rather than experience, is the foundation of knowledge

socialism a political theory that states the production and exchange of goods should be regulated by the government

scepticism the theory that knowledge is impossible

subjective a judgment that is influenced by opinions

theism the belief that a divine being exists

universal including, relating to, or affecting all members of a group being considered

utilitarianism the moral theory that an action is right if it creates the greatest happiness for the greatest number of people

Index

Rachel Poulton is a writer, photographer and educator, who writes about philosophy, history, folklore, and the land. She loves to explore life's mysteries, and lives among the rolling Downs of Sussex, UK.

The publisher would like to thank the following people for their help in the production of this book: Polly Goodman for proofreading; Helen Peters for the index; Shubhdeep Kaur and Rituraj Singh for picture research; Nityanand Kumar for hi-res assistance; Ann Cannings for additional design; and Lynne Murray for picture library assistance.

Picture credits